The Layers Beneath

Revealing

Tamara M. Peacock

BookLeaf Publishing
India | USA | UK

Presentation by *BookLeaf Publishing*

Web: www.bookleafpub.com

E-mail: info@bookleafpub.com

ISBN: 9789363313446

First edition 2024

This book is dedicated to all of the parts within me. It is also dedicated to all my experiences that have brought me to today. I also tribute this book to my highest power which is greater than me. I would like to acknowledge all the different 12-Step programs that create a safe and loving space who struggle with any sort of addiction.

ACKNOWLEDGEMENT

Dear Tam (Inner Child),

You are a gift and a part of your True Parent. I am sorry I can not see you freely right now. I know you are there. You have always been there. I feel you and I hear you at times. Please be patient with me. I am willing and doing the work to unbury you. I am sorry I have abandoned you. I am a work in progress and always will be. I commit to you that I will continue to be willing to the process of healing. I want to be gentle and patient with myself. It is going to take time. I am working on loving all of us. Even those parts that felt the need to protect you from our family. They worked hard because they had to. I am working hard to be the loving parent you have always deserved. I love you, Tam. I am also fearful of you in the same breath. We haven't been acquainted for so many years. I will continue to challenge myself to overcome that fear over time.

I want to say thank you to every single experience and person who has been in my life. No matter if it has been for an extended period of time, or just in passing. Each moment has brought me to this point in my life. All the situations were meant for me to become my true self. There is a reason for every situation, experience, and pain. I would like to acknowledge my progression to my freedom.

PREFACE

My name is Tamara Michelle Peacock. I am an adult child who grew up in a family of dysfunction and alcoholism. This is my second book. I have many creative writing pieces that I want to release and share with others. I write to tap into my creative side as well as to purge the trauma the younger parts of me endured. I am on a healing journey and these writings are a critical part of that journey. The writings are parts of me that were unspoken for decades. Finding my voice and ways to express grief, pain, hurt, fear, anger, and new emotions I am getting acquainted with. It is incredible to see how dysfunction affected my life and the life of my family. The silence, the boxes, the confinement, and hope expressed in the writings. They are my passion, my pain, my sight, my growth, and development. It is an honor to be able to share it with you!

"Highest Power"

Not often confident in your power and existence
I know you are there
I see your strength
Cylinder tornados touching down
Wiping out towns and cities
Wildfires spreading like bed bugs
Earthquakes from 2.6 to 10 on the Richter Scale
Oh so formable
Passionate like Mike Tyson in the ring
Willing to take more than an ear
Destructive and demanding
Responding to the behaviors of us humans
Convincing the world or at least attempting too
Some keep their hearts and eyes closed
Minds distracted
Unwilling to hear the message
Sacrificing the welfare of all for the Green $$

I see you
I can also feel your presence
Watching the miracles of life
Plants blooming
The rain falling from the sky
The circle of life
Providing naturally
No need for human help

You are my creator
Master of the final plan
Always present
No matter how far I attempt to run away
Consuming myself with people, places, and things
Not sure what to do
Working on doing nothing
How foreign
Trying to control someone or something
The program says to do nothing and turn it over
I will leave room for you to do your thing
Instead of being in your way
The process of trusting something that isn't tangible
Fighting the program's instincts

“R&B”

Attraction and addiction
Lead by the latter
Resemblance of the family
Pick me or me pick you
I want a new set of parents
Two fathers or another single mother
Any will do
Just do for me what they couldn’t
Needing loving, safety, and security
Are you up for the challenge?

Fix me….I beg….please
Adult by number and appearance
Emotions and actions are child-driven
Make decisions for me…please
I will resent you later
I will be fine
Acronym: frustrated, insecure, neurotic, and emotional
The picture looks familiar
I will resent you later

Test of your love and commitment were regular
Manipulation and attempted control on both sides of the street
How does that work?

It doesn't
Tug of war
If you did not do what I wanted, I would
abandon you
Withdrawal
Both sides standing firm
Eventually, one side would cave

R&B were not the only ones

R&B, not the type of music
The type of people
Similar to my family of origin
Playing the same notes on the piano
It needs a tune-up
But what does an intune piano sound like?
No clue
I choose the out-of-tune that is familiar

Deserving every sharp cord ringing in my ears
Developing a tolerance for insanity
Choosing to stay put….
Please
Don't tune the piano
It is just fine
(Frustrated, insecure, neurotic, and emotional)

I choose it
A willing participant in the game

Volleying the ball over the net
Hoping they would not hit the ball
Back over to me

Take all the tennis balls
Keep them forever
I don’t want them anymore

"Casket Jumper"

Monetarily valuable piece of equipment
Costing thousands of dollars
Break bank accounts
Headstone
Plots for the earth
They are not biodegradable
Funeral expenses
Wake services
It often seemed too much
There was mourning and regret
Consuming the family, the church, and the spirits
The body cold and solid
No longer a naturally flowing human
Skin full of formaldehyde-based solution
Just a shell of one's self

The real show begins at the place where you worshiped
Somber and sad
I saw you hop in the casket
As if you were going to resuscitate the corpse
It looked like regret
What a production
The Oscar is yours

Alive they were resented and disliked
What were the things you wish you could say
now that they are gone?
Would they behave differently with a re-do?
As an observer, at a young age
It was so confusing
When they were alive, those affections did not
exist

The family tradition is the performance at the
best level
Exaggerated the reality of the insanity
Either way, it was never the truth
The masks were being worn
Disguising all the things that were not allowed
to be spoken about
So jump in that casket
Close the lid
Put them both on the ground
See if that changes the past!!

“Sleep”

Deprived of it for so long
So many things happened to us when we were in the state of resting the body and mind
Never a break from the madness
Hands violating our physical being
Where were we to find safety?
As a child/teen, we found it in our head
Some of the time
Leaving the body
Fantasizing about other things
Convincing ourselves that we weren’t worthy of healthy and unconditional love
“We must have been adopted”
This must be how love is shown?
It never felt like love
Always scary; even as we became older
Restless slumber
Hearing the voices of the adults in the homes
Sexualized by the family
Exposed to the conversations
The pornography
The glares and looks from the grown-up as the body developed
Forced to shower with you as a teenager
No privacy in the bathroom or bedroom
My body was scarred

My bed was a torture chamber of confusion
The shower/bath exposed my whole body to the perpetration
Even clothed, I could feel the eyes and hands on me
Nervous system armed and ready for the unknown and confusing feelings
Not able to go through the natural processes of development as a child/teenager
Now a 50-ish year old women
Reparenting those parts that were unloved by insane people
Punishing
Deteriorating from the inside out
Cancer
Mental Health issues
Addiction
Abuse
Suffering
They were unable to give me any different
I deserved more
I put down the torch
No longer willing to carry it

Sleep is my friend
I will embrace it
Bask in it
Rest in it
And find my peace

I am safe
I am no longer that child/teen
They can no longer hurt me (us)
Any of us
I am your loving parent in training

Our higher power is uniquely ours
We do not have to believe or conform
We will and can create our path
And we are
I love you Tam
I love you Tamara
I love you my highest power
I thank you all! We are here
We are becoming free

“Dear Pumpkin Pussface Peacock aka-Triple P”

Orange and white
Thick and sassy
Thick meaning beautiful
Not cat shaming at all
Vibrant with lots of personality
Selective of who you wanted to spend your time with
Describing qualities of you
Reminds me of me
The brightest and most unique pair of eyes
Super sharp claws
I could not bring myself to get them declawed
It looked painful
You were born that way
So I would not and did not
But ouch
Natural tool for protection
I still have scars that remind me of you
In good ways, with a sprinkle of pain
It was worth every minute
Despite my frustrations at times
You are a part of me
Pumpkin with the bright orange color in your coat

My snuggle and cuddle bunny
I looked back at some of the photos of you
Playing in that Bob Evans brown bag
Hiding in boxes
Laying near or on me, and often touching me
Unconditional love without ever having to ask
Such a great companion, family member, and my baby girl
Always and forever a part of me
I do wish I could have spent more time with you towards the end
I have some healthy guilt behind it
I did my best to show you love and care
You will always have a special place in my heart and soul
Two peas in a pod
Made for each other
I didn't think I could find my match
Then you caught my eye
They let us play
And you were the ONE
Never thought I would love a cat
My grandfather was deathly afraid of cats
You were protective of your territory and that included me
Liked a few and disliked many
Sounds like your momma….me
You are missed and deeply loved
I hated to see you suffer

I am glad you are free from any pain
Certainly liveda full life
We were a great team
Stubborn and always gonna do it your way
I can relate!!! LOL
What a bond and friendship
You helped me grow and practice my parenting skills
Never confident in my parental ability
You, sunshine, and the other animals were proof
It was my pleasure to be your momma
Please forgive me for my shortcomings as a human
Love always, Your momma

“Support”

The road was very rocky
Boulders and potholes to my left and to my right
Was it ever smooth sailing?
Who was the support?
All alone (at least it felt that way)
Stranded
Trying to find my way
Afraid to ask for help
Feeling like I had to figure it out
Asking for help meant weakness and a deficit
So manipulation and attempting to control
became my tools
Still seeking others to “fix” my broken parts
Or so I thought

"Just US"

Taking up more and more space
To be seen, heard, and felt
Voice that has been lost for so long
Mouth bonded with an unrequested gag
Black ball with black leather straps
Reinforced with steel buckles
Arm tied behind my back with the tightest rope
Leaving scars around my wrist and face
Unseen to most

Still able to hear my own murmurs
Ever so quiet
Bundled up in tight rubber bands
Getting thicker and thicker over the years
All of us and me
Ready to shoot outside of my skills like a rocket
Shedding the coat of armor
The shell of my soul
Holds the scars and pain

Ready to expose our purest form
Never seen with my own eyes
So curious and enthusiastic
Bouncy, flexible, durable, encompassing lots of
energy and force with each bounce

My arm is the lever used to create more
intensity, frequency, and height
Projecting to the stars, the moon, and the sun
No more darkness and fancy masks
Denial is left behind
The reality of me begins with us
Holding hands
Feeling free
Precious and beautiful
For all the world to see, but more importantly
I can finally see myself!!!

"Value"

Worthiness
In the eyes of the beholder
Can be decided by others
Different to see inwards
Early-day impressions tainted the view
Believed in one's own depreciation
Learned at an early age
To disbelieve the truth
Born in light, love, blessings, and gratitude
It was given to me freely
The center of my core
Still existing
Hidden behind the walls of survival
Caged behind the brick walls
Light peeking through the small holes of hope
Ready for the sledgehammer to be permanently
attached
To my fists
Beating down the lies throughout the years
The blame, shame, and guilt from others
Feeling my soul
Wings spread wide
Fully intact
No longer clipped

"I See You"

Intensity from your eyes
Intentful and gentle
Playing close attention
Desiring to see what's really there
The depths of the soul
Intimacy in its highest form
Voice ever so soothing
Offering comfort and understanding
Spitting realness
Sharing vulnerability and rawness
Breathing deeply with sighs in between
Seeing your chest rise up and down slowly
Your body relaxes even more
The body language speaks loudly
Attentive to yourself and others
Leading with kindness and humor
Wanting to know more…
What's your story?
Impactful and frightening
Exposing self and seeking exposure from others
Humane and tender
Considerate and soft
Your grin and smile are like sunshine
Brightness in your eyes sharing love and peace
I see you D
You are a gift of God

"I Remember the Pink"

I remember the pink halter short set
It was not my favorite
Tied behind my neck
Tight!!
Leaving a mark right at the top of my spine
The short part hit me right at mid-thigh
The texture was fuzzy a little
Reminded me of summer
Apartment in Oregon
Laying on the couch for a nap
Nap time was not my favorite time
You at my feet
A grin on your face like the joker
I drift to sleep
Waking up to a bodily response
Disheveled hair
My pink halter untied
You still at my feet
A look of shame was a cloud of you and I
I get up to use the restroom
Thinking I wet myself
What had happened to me?

“ENOUGH”

When is enough enough?
Who determines the value of enough?
How does one achieve enough?
What does enough look like?
Why is enough not enough?

I say… I AM ENOUGH!!!
Love me

“Pieces”

Inclusive with all my parts
All-encompassing
Connecting all together
They is me
I am she/her
He/him and them

Identified at birth as female based on gender
Who I am is fluid
Flowing like a warm ocean of water
Keeping myself hydrated
Accepting all the facets of myself
The puzzle pieces were hidden
Now putting them together
Aligning the edges
Carefully taking my time

Many thoughts attempting to separate the pieces
Still pushing on despite the old tapes
Playing in my head

New neurological connections being created
Formulating a new way of thinking
Embracing all the beautiful loving molecules
The cells developing in a healthy way
Living more as a whole person

Out of the box
Free at last

“Void”

The fridge was never empty
My belly was always full
The body had beautiful garments
Feet in the latest brands
The external looked the part
No visible marks or bruises noticeable to others
Voids were unseen and unheard
The adults wanted it that way

The soul was ruptured and deprived
Yearning for peace, love, hope, and safety
The ‘walking wounded’ and no one really knew
The mask covered the entire body
Smile on broad
Head held high

Laughing to hide the suffering
Camouflaging to fit in
Army fatigues to blend in
A chameleon in the forest
Tip-toeing through the minefields

Alert alert…
Take cover
Build the walls
Barricade yourself

High to the sky
Keep them out or else

A lonely road behind the walls
But who can be trusted?
The neighbors, family, teachers? Who?
It is too risky to trust and feel
I chose the walls
They won't fail me
Or will they?

"Gender Roles"

G.I. Joes
Legos
Building blocks and linking logs
Chemistry sets and baseball caps
Visors to help shield the sun
The race track my father introduced me too
Puzzles and board games
Judo and basketball
Softball and kickball
Climbing trees and playing four-square
Some of the many pleasures of my inner child/teen
They say girls wear dresses and cross the legs at the knees or ankles
You behave like a bull dyke
Little girls play with barbies, make-up, and easy-bake ovens
I love easy-bake ovens
Barbies got the military cut and limbs removed
Me no like
Enjoyed the custom black raggedy Ann and Andy dolls

I feel demeaned by these words and stringent gender roles
I want to play sports, climb trees, garden, play board games, and play with toys that bring me joy; not your joy

My dear child, I hear you loud and clear
You have a voice, likes, dislikes, and choice
I encourage you to explore healthy activities and games you like
I support and love you
You are heard
Wanna go outside and play curveball or shoot some hoops?

“Heartbroken”

Although I never wanted to think
I just wanted to hate
Watch you suffer from a distance
Far enough away so you couldn’t see or want to touch me
Your touch was never soothing
It was sick, shaming, harming, and unsafe

Never wanting to feel these feelings
Did everything imaginable to avoid and deny
My truth
The truth is…
I trusted you
I loved you
I believed in you
I hoped you would love me in the way I deserved

Those things never happened and it is painful
I deserved and deserve love, support, and protection
Since you were unable to provide them
I am willing to learn and implement these basic needs

It is difficult to accept you did not know any
better
But the truth is, how could you have done
anything different when you did not know
different?

“Balance”

Learning how to ride a bike
Practicing flying a kite
Doing a handstand
Juggling are acts of balance

Distribution of weight
Steady positioning
Prioritizing things of importance
Use to look like a squirrel chasing its tail
Running around in circles
Stuck in the same position

My life in shambles
Cycle of destruction
Feeling isolated and alone
Never wanting anyone to know
Self-sufficiency was practiced to prove myself
But to whom?

There is no balance
Often falling off the tightrope
Now…. I have some clarity of what matters the most
It is me, it is a power greater than myself, and it is love
New perspective on myself (past and present)

No longer willing to throw myself under the bus
I am learning to give to myself

"Consent"

It implies a right or voice
Does it mean freedom
Of choice and selection?
Dictionary.com gives the definition
Society shapes its meaning differently

Children are not allowed to give consent
A parent/guardian must be their voice
What rights do children have?
Who protects them from their families and
perpetrators?
Do people really care?
"People" stands for the ones in charge of making
the laws and enforcing them

Over the years, history continues to repeat itself
It may appear to be different
Just smoke and mirrors
Human trafficking, sexual assaults, rapes, and
incest are the quiet secrets
Happening to men, women, children, and
transgender people

Where are their voices?
Not in the courts or on the juries
Not in the tabloids

The victims are being revictimized in court and society
Blamed for the choices of others

Their stories, if told, diminished and/or hushed
Where are their choices?
Disposed of like trash
Discarded and never thought of
"They got what they deserved"
Injustice and a slap in the face

Immigrants coming to America for opportunity
Traded for coins
Pimped out, drugged up, and murdered
No identity

"The American Dream"
What a nightmare

“Whirlwind”

Swooping in like a hawk inching closer to its
prey
Lifting trees from their roots
Swifty and steady
I heard you last night
Seeping through the cracks in this old house
Making your presence known
More powerful than any human being
Destructive and soothing at the same time
Calm and ferocious
Moving tons of water
Demolishing buildings
Blowing the fall leaves all over the yard
You are a force
A product of my Higher Power
The example of my powerlessness I need
Gently rolling across my cheek
Two limbs from the neighbor’s tree
Denting up my car
I feel you
I hear you
I see what you can do

“Mirror mirror”

Looking in the mirror can feel torturous
I often would look past myself
Avoiding making eye contact
If I glare too long, what emotions might come up?
The fear had the better of me

Excluding self-worth and confidence
Broad shoulders
And strong physique
Thinking physical strength and intimidation could protect me

Hiding myself with loud belly laughs and jokes
Having high judgment of myself and others
Pretending I had my shit together
Accommodating yet passive-aggressive
People pleasing to the point of resentment

Educated by textbooks
Performing at my highest level
Athlete and scholar
Ducking behind props, trophies, and degrees
The smiles masking the self-hatred

A suit of armor
A titanium shield
Impenetrable to self and others
Rejecting self and others
Abandonment of self and others

Deep in the dark within myself
Secrets suffocating me
Hurt, shame, guilt, and blame
Laying on top of my youthful self
The self from the original single mold
Finding it hard to breathe
The weight on my chest is crushing my ribs and
internal organs
I inhale quickly
I will be crushed alive
It will be my last breath

"Mint Condition"

If the plants could talk…
What would they say?
The small and tall cacti
Needles sharp like razors
Why did my mother love those painful things?
I was responsible for watering and helping her move them
OUCH….

I was a nervous child, so I often hurt my arm or hand on the cacti
Bleeding and shaking in fear
Looking over my shoulder
Bracing myself for impact
The prick from the plants became my friend through the years
As did other forms of physical pain
Self-inflicted
Gave me a rush and allowed me to be present in the pain
Even just for the moment
It became an addiction
To the point that the pain disappeared
It became pleasure
Sitting in the tattoo chair is calming
Needles penetrating my skin

Releasing some of the internal
pain….temporarily
Sitting as still as a marble statue
No screaming, jumping, flinching, or passing out
Stoic
Steady
Sedated
My body being washed over with endorphins
and a sense of relief
Thank you cacti
You helped save my life

Wicker Peacock chair
So beautiful and delicate
Durable with all its unique sounds when sat
upon
Prized possession in the house
Pier 1 was her favorite home decor store
Definitely not a playground for a child
The smell is a memory that fills my nasal
passage
Woods
Sandalwood
Cottonwood
Cedarwood
Incents
Maybe even hints of sage
Serene in the midst of chaos
Peacock feathers in a vase
Vibrant and gorgeous
The family crest

“Homeland”

A place with open land and streams of
crystal-clear waters
Trees and honeybees
Butterflies hovering over the flowers
Pollinating and spreading love
The air is crisp and clean
Foraging the lands for nutrition

The space is shared with the wildlife
Utmost respect for all in the space
Preserving and cultivating life through the
universe
Using natural resources sparingly
Replenishing the land with crops
Shared with family and the animals

Chickens on the range
Providing cage-free eggs
Able to roam the land
Sunflowers as tall as medium trees
Bright yellow
Seen a mile away

Interactions are pure and wholesome
Breathing clean, fresh, and crisp air
Deep inhale

Gradual exhale
Taking time to smell the roses
Feeling grounded in my Higher power and true
self
Not a fear
Just peace and love
The highest form of connection

Running barefoot through the creek
Fishing in the river
Cooking over an open fire
Sharpening the cooking knives with stone
Living off the land

Minimal hustle and bustle
Silent and tranquil
The environment always wrapping its arms
around me ever so tightly

“Kindness”

Out in the crowd I saw you
On your best behavior
Smiling brighter than the sun
Teeth white and glistening from the beams
Shaking hands
Using your manners
Polite and kind
Hugging people and laughing loudly
Who is this person I see?

Totally different at our residence
How could I decide which was real or my
reality?
Utterly confused and astonished
Questioning myself
As if it was me that caused your actions behind
closed doors

Strangers were respected and shown admiration
I did not recall seeing that side of you
Facid and fantasy island
Why could I not receive goodness?
This happiness
The energy that looked loving
What was wrong with me?

The children in me always thought they were not good enough
The loving parent in training and practice says
"It was never about you. It was about them"
Pass on a terrible disease generation after generation
Projecting what was done to them onto you
You were and are always enough

I know your pain and anger
Rightful emotions
I am here for you and so is the God of your choice
We will take care of you

You are love
Always have been love
Never a thought or a doubt
You are a child of your Higher Power
You are not a mistake
Kindness and light are and have always been inside you

I see you
I embrace you
I am here for you

I love you Tam

“The Pain Ends”

The pain was once unbearable
Wrapping its cold hands around my neck and
squeezing ever so tightly
Almost taking my breath completely away
Destroying my mind, body, soul, and beautiful
spirit
Nails digging into my tender flesh
Attempting to draw blood

As I shut my eyes
I feel the warm breeze across my pores
Hairs standing up like a military soldier
Opening my eyes to the bright sun
The clouds look so fluffy
I want to jump on them as I listen to the song
“Jump Around” by House of Pain

My heart beats faster in the most peaceful way
Those hands are slowly loosening their grip
Seeing native birds flying in the sky
Chirping at one another
“The hands slide completely off my neck”
Energy and love consume my insides
A smile on my face

Dreams became abundant and visible
Seeing myself through the eyes of my Higher
Power
Challenging that strangulation from the past
Feeling compassion for the pain and the people
who initially caused it

Starting to cry
My inner children feel warm and safe
The very first time in decades
The critical voice diminishing with every breath
Screaming on the inside
But the scream getting quieter and quieter

I tell them all to rest my family
It is a new day
It is a beautiful day
We are everything we were created to be

“Rest Your Mind”

What is rest, little one?
We do not know.
I am here to introduce you
It was what you did not get, but deserved

The amount of worry you have endured was not yours to carry
I am here to tell you
You were born as peace, love, and light
It is all still here; just as it ever was
No one or thing could ever take it from you
I feel your pain
It is real and true
Nothing you ever deserved in your young lives

It is time to get some rest
You all have worked hard
To help keep us all safe
You did more than any child should have to do
I thank you
For your courage, bravery and creativity
Crafting ways to preserve your essence
Fighting every day of our lives

I am here to take the load off of your shoulders
I can do it
I will not be perfect
I will be with willingness, effort, and the support
of the power greater than me

You are overdue for freedom
So let's get to it
Grabbing it with both hands
Holding on tight
All the things that happened to us
Does not define us
We are not the trauma or abuse
You are not a mistake
And never were
You were made by the greatest power
We are a product of joy, love, and kindness
It is ok to put down the fears, worry, and
resentment
It does not serve our peace
We deserve it
What once was is in the past
The present is now
And the future is ours to enjoy
You have earned it

“Your Shit”

I reek of your
words
Actions

It is yours, not mine
No matter how much you slather it on
Your name is all over it
Smells of fear, blame, shame, and guilt
It is still yours
Not mine

Throwing dirt on top of it to keep it on my skin
Beating it into my pores with the belt and
switches
Rubbing it in my hair like shampoo
Spitting it out of your mouth into my ears
It’s still yours
Not mine

Daily reminders
Weekly insults
Disease spewing out of your body
The flies gravitating to it
It is yours
Not mine

It hurt to hear

I internalized it
Wearing it like a badge of honor
What honor?
It is still yours
Not mine

Looking in the mirror
Turning away because it feels uncomfortable
The reflection was never really me
It was all the lies I was told about myself
A suit of steel
Trying to reject the shit that hit my skin
It is yours
Not mine

Years of wondering
Believing
And digesting
All the bogus tongue lashings
Never kept me down or from being hopeful
Deep down I knew it was not mine
It was always your shit
I now dispose of it, bit by bit
Little by little

I am not your shit
You were not your shit either
But I do not think you were able to figure that
out.

“Interracial Relationships”

Race has been tracked for centuries
Separating the human races into groups
Dividing the line in the sand with segregation
Some lighter nationalities placed as the authority
The darker the skin, the less value
Significant in many insignificant ways
Culture is important
Traditions and customs are unique to specific groups

Identities and lives have been taken because of ethnic differences
Slander and slurs
Oppression and systematic separation
Deviant blueprints to split
Television shows depicting darker-skinned people as animals
Beasts to be contained

Comments like “my best friend is black,” I can not be racist
“I have a gay friend”—I can not be homophobic
My family calling caucasian people crackers and honkies
Or being referred to as “white devils”
The judgments exist in all the groups

Fear, intimidation, and wealth allow the minority
to make life-altering decisions for all humans
Laws encouraged to allow a population of
people to determine what a female can or cannot
do with her own body in 2023
Look how far we have come, they say
Not very

Rallies promoting white supremacy in cities
Promoting the superiority of one race over
others

Same-raced groups annihilating each other with
violence and drugs

Slum lords and unfair housing inequity

How far have we really come?

"Black and White"

They teach black and white
Right or wrong
Large or small
Fat or skinny
Tall or short
Always a comparison
Then labeling one better or greater than the other
Stigma attached to anything that is not received by others

The trap of self-destruction
Falling down the rabbit hole of desiring to be accepted
By who?
Social media cranking up the heat
Beauty defined by others
Less about how we see ourselves
Comparing and contrasting
Minimal individuality

A snip here, a tuck there
One mold for all individuals
Uniqueness diminishes
Self-love……what is that?
What others say it is?
Or my decision?
It is a slippery slope

Encouraged to fit in the template
Coloring in the lines
Or else, it is bad or ugly

Says who?
Built to stand out
Not to fit in
Individual and original

Breaking the container
Embracing what was bestowed upon me
Behind the fear, insecurities, and judgment
Lies everything I am meant to be
Born authentic and pure
Until……

Stigma, ridicule, criticism, belittling, and projections
Shoved that beautiful human into a box
Walls of pewter
Protecting those precious parts
Just to navigate and survive all the insanity

It does not have to be what it once was
A leaf can be turned over
The sun can shine brighter
Light in all things
Super and powerful
Able to shine even in the darkest of times.

“I Don’t Wanna”

Disguising myself with a shield
A feathered mask
One with leather and pearls
Another that was scary like Frankenstein after surgery
Fused together with all types of parts
Anything to hide behind
No one could ever know
The family secrets must be kept
Till death do us part
DEATH

The denial was digging my grave, slowly but surely
6,000 feet deep
I have had the shovel since the early days
Not understanding why I was digging
But I dug
Deeper and deeper
Burrowing any trace of the original gangster of self

I attempted all the things and people to obtain “love”
Learning to sacrifice myself, wants, and needs
Just for a glimpse of hope

Thinking I could deny the pain away
Finger point at others
Making fun
Criticizing a look, word, an appearance
I learned from the best teachers

Chasing my tail to get people to like me
Agree with me
See me, but not the real me
A shell of myself

Layers of lies
Untruth after untruth
Smiling and saying " I am fine"
"How's your mom?"
She's fine!!!

"Your mom is so great"
Grinning that fake grin and saying thank you
In my mind, wondering why I did not get to see those sides of her
Oh yeah…..
She was wearing her mask too
Even when she was hurting me, she had it on
It had to be the mask of someone who hurt and violated her.

"Solution"

Like a leaf falling off a tree
The wind blowing my hair
Your fingers softly gliding against my skin
Warm like the rays of the sun

Offering calmness, serenity, and peace
No rush; no hurry
Just resting in the moment
Staying present and current
No dwelling in the past
Or planning every second of the future

Being still
Sitting with myself
Wrapping my loving arms around me
Tears of joy
Words of love and understanding
Whispering…"I love you" to myself
Meaning it and believing it

“Resistance”

Hurdles and obstacles
Ups and downs
Rounds and rounds
Pushing and pulling

No matter what it is, I was going to get it down
I am persistent
Bound and determined
To make things happen
Good, not good, or indifferent
Give me a task or challenge
I will deliver
Performing at the top level
At any cost
What an expensive price
To pay…
Abandoning myself

Now it is my time
To be able to fully shine
Showing myself love, compassion, patience, and kindness
Foreign ideas and feelings
But this too, shall be done

"Trust"

What a great idea!
Desirable concept
What does it look like?
What does it feel like?
I am unknowing

A child growing up with people who were responsible for me
Not knowing how to display trust or give it
The little ones were the ones to suffer
Carrying the lack of trust
Into our adult lives

Establishing entanglements with a minimal level of trust
Or even confidence in oneself or others
How can I trust you, when I do not trust myself?
For me, it can not happen

Expecting people to abandon me
Or me beating them to the punch of abandonment
Lack of connectivity with others and self
Alone on the island
Fearful
Without a map, paddle, or boat
Such a lonely place

“Own Person”

What does Own mean to me?
Own=Mine
Person=Individual
Sounds freeing
Independent
Self=me
What happens in life that we veer away from the self?
Own person is so personal
We have so many similarities
But we also have important and unique differences
They define who we are authentically

Why is the world so fearful of authentic people?
Why is there so much attempted control over other people?
Why can’t I be who I really am?
I will give you my reasons….
Trauma, fear, people-pleasing, codependency, denial, dysfunction, and lack of recovery

If I want to be my own person
I will need personal connection and continued support from my highest power
Being responsible for me

Rewiring my neural pathways
Time and patience
It is possible and I deserve it
It is now up to me to know who I am and want to be
No one else has the authority, unless I give it to them

“Threshold of Pain”

High tolerance of you and all in between
Created from trauma of all sorts
Ways to deal with the discomfort and suffering
Willing to do many things to relieve it
Damn….

Manifesting more pain because the feeling still exists
Engraved in my tissues
Not only in my brain
Also in my body
Physical, mental, and emotional pain

Suffering internally
Agony stemming from out of my control
Increasing the endorphins in my body
Seeking relief from outside entities and my own internal drugstore

Learning it is an inside job
Working through the pain is not painless
It takes courage to be honest about the pain and where it comes from
New ways to work through it
Actually feeling the sensations of the mind and body

Staying in my body, instead of trying to run
from my whole self

Finding my True Parent
Learning I can manage me
Not my surroundings or others
Digging deep seeing the most awful memories
Releasing the secrets
Applying ointment and bandages as needed

All the experiences are part of me
They do not have to define me
Minimizing the false self
Moving closer to the true me

No longer punishing myself and others
Owning my shit
Engaging my resources and support system
Providing self-love to me
Putting myself first
Becoming my own loving parent

“Humor”

Gut busting
Pant pissing
Tears flowing down the cheeks
Unable to breathe
Dopamine swirling

Amusing laughter
Excitement and joy
Tension reduction
Stress release
Making light of life

Taking a minute to us wit
Becoming an actor
Instead of reacting to things out of my control
Taking full advantage of the moments
Breathing relief once it over

Delightful and warm
Spreading the contagion to others
Brightening up someone’s day
Just from a smile, laugh, or humor

Traveling rapidly through the body
Moving through the air
My ecosystem seems less combative
Glimpses of peace and tranquility
A little bit of laughter goes a long way

“Diamond”

An element of carbon
Formed under extreme pressure
Difficult to destroy
Shines brightly
The stone of my zodiac
Reflecting light into rainbows
Representing love, strength, and health

Diamonds have been adorned for centuries by all types of people
Flashing in grills on teeth and cars
Glistening with richness
Costing more than gold

One of the precious stones of the earth
Strong like me
Created under intense pressure
I came from the womb not expecting how chaotic, insane, and unsafe the environment would be
Just a few words to describe my connection to this stone
Extreme elements and environmental influences

The tough exterior protects my beating heart
Full of love, strength, and health

The things that represent my truest self
The one that is connected to my higher power
The original me

"Wholeness"

Piece by piece
Cell by cell
Never-ending
Muscle beginning

I was born complete
Along the way
Those who looked out for me
Were fragmented and surviving
Living the best way they could

Attempting to do things "differently"
Unconsciously repeating history
Generation after generation
Parent to child
Year after year

How could anyone expect a different outcome?
Who spends time talking about PTSD in all its forms?
Shattered hearts
Broken spirits
Control and defenses

It was never a thing we talked about
It was swept under the rug

Just pray about it
Their god will fix it

Put on a smile and pretend
The wholeness got buried under the chipped
bones
And torn ligaments

Fuck…. that sure does hurt

"Letting Go"

I have pretended the majority of my life to know
what the words meant
How to do it
Failing at every attempt
Just running
Hiding behind others

Avoiding myself and my feelings
Never thinking I deserved to be heard
To be free
TO feel like I have a voice
Bumping my head over and over again

Feeling like a hamster in the wheel
Going round and round
So many circles
Definitely got my steps in
Right back to the same spot I started from

Endless insanity
The quote is so true
Behaving the same
Expecting a different outcome

Gracious, how painful the familiar was
Frightened by the unfamiliar
Drowning in my own fear, shame, and guilt
But was it all mine?

“Sun Is Shining (Sunshine)”

The word, the name, the meaning, and the action
All fill me with so much happiness
It brings me warmth and light to the darkest of
days
It has come to me through a fur baby
She has been gone for many years now
She lives within me
Bringing me companionship
I was able to spend 14 years with her

Not only does my highest power bring sunshine
Through the earth
Allowing vegetation to grow
Living things to be fed
People able to get their vitamin D

The sunshine brightens the mood
Encourages movement, fun, and enjoyment
It makes me want to connect with nature
Long walks at the park
Growing some of my favorite foods
Greens, okra, lettuce, tomatoes, beans, and
cucumbers

Oh I hear my belly growling
Yearning for the chloroplast from the green veggies
Tasting like my grannies
Bittersweet, flavorful, and juicy

Mother Earth has offered up so many blessings
Allowing for nourishment
Renewable resources like the sun
Supplies what we need
I thank you for all you have given

"Shame"

Humiliation is embarrassing
Causing great pain
And even shame
Wrongful behavior
Intending to create pain
And discomfort

Does not feel good
Or sound fun
It is a wonder why and how
So many of us distribute and receive it
From those closest and farthest away
From a circle of connectivity

Shame has existed for generations
Decade after decade
Belittling at such a deep level
Emotional torment

Evolution can and does change the world
Including people
With willingness or without consent
How much would it take
To be kind
To be self-aware and dealing with all the secrets
Peeling back the layers of the onion

Refusing the projection of my hurt and insecurities

Giving compliments
Smiling
Living my authentic, joyous, and happy life
How contagious could this concept be?

Better days are possible

“The Eyes”

The gateway to the soul, they say
I can see through you
You have a smile on your face
But your eyes are bleeding
Sharp daggers piercing the pupil
They are dilated
Seeing you as your present self
Wanting to believe it is a figment of my
imagination
My eyes see you
And my flesh feels you
My heart is shredded
The brain is mush
Emotions are limited
Constant flight, freeze, fight, and fawn
Where was I to go?
At every exit, there was a trap
Felt caged, raw, mentally and physically
tortured, mutilated, and permanently scarred
A fragment of the pain in my heart, mind, and
soul

"Rich Life"

Rich originally looked like the Benjamins $
Able to afford any and everything I wanted
At what cost?
In this country, the mighty dollar is king
The more the merrier
Greed presents itself around the corner
Rich has changed for me
Personal safety and security are the most important
My basic needs and essentials provided for
A roof over my head that has a strong foundation
Nourishment for my mind, body, and soul is key for me
Ability to take care of all my parts…
Financial security is a plus
Medical insurance and a good PCP
People in my life who I can have an interdependent relationship with
A connection with my highest power and true self
Trips to places on the bucket list with people I love
This is my new kind of rich

“I”

A single word with a single letter
Encompassing so much
Standing alone in the world
But never alone
Capital, lowercase, and pronoun
Representing each individual independently
If I choose
What a concept!
Autonomy
Identity
Decisions and choices
Determined by “I”
Sounds like a fictional story
I could not relate
I felt singular on an island in the Pacific Ocean
Basic needs barely met
Waking up everyday wishing for connection,
love and individuality
How was I to define myself?
Invisible to the world and more importantly to
myself
So I thought
Sometimes feeling unreal
Not tangible, impalpable
A shell of myself
That was then

Now “I” is me and I am I
ENOUGH
A creation full of love and abundance bestowed upon me at birth

“World with THEM”

Is it a sphere?
Is it flat?
Right or Wrong?
Loving or hateful?
What is real?
Do they care?
Who made the rules and the boxes?

So many expectations and laws
Never satisfied or good enough
They said
I say
Fuck you and them
Stone throwers from a glass house
Full of secrets and indiscretions
Moral and immoral
How dare you?
Unsafe and insane

Facades reflecting off of glass buildings
Seeing people, places, and things for what they
are
At least 50% terrible
100% terrible in my house
50% is generous and far-fetched

They have been scarred and passed on the scars
Agonizing in pain and despair
How could you?
Why would you?

Never to be trusted
Difficult to have healthy relationships
Self-love
Peace

Until…..NOW

“Darling Eyes”

Bright as the sun shining at its highest point
Deep with a beautiful brown hue
With a darker brown
A black ring around the pupil
They tell the story
Most will never know or care to know

Seeing the truth for a short period of time
Before the “Big people” made their debut
When I first saw you I had the most confidence
Everyone was loved and innocent
I was safe, just for a few moments
Full of happiness, joy, and innate trust

Once upon a time
40 plus years ago
Life became very dark
Like their eyes
No longer seeing the love and light
Pain and torture pierced from behind their eyes
The light had dimmed in our eyes
Hard to light up the earth
Hiding behind all the masks

I have hated you
But could never stop loving you
I am so glad you are gone
Good riddance
P.S. I still love you
No longer have to fear you

"Smile"

Lights up a room
My mother made sure my teeth were
well-groomed
Regular cleanings/xrays/and repairs
One year I had 12 or more cavities
Sneaking candy and other sweets
Barely brushing my teeth
Momma was not happy

Compliments came regularly
Your teeth are so white
Your smile is so beautiful
It seems to soften people up
Bring a bit of joy to others

Greeting people with a smile
Helps to put their guard down at times
Laughter is a form of medicine
Defenseless, allowing people in
Vulnerability

What does it hurt?
Me?
You?
An innocent exchange between people
Disarming a mood quickly

Kind and friendly
Another expression of love
Keeping it simple

It is a treasure to see the power of uniqueness
Gentleness
Giving something away that does not cost a thing
Free and hopefully painless
A gift
Gratitude

“Connections”

C=Conversation
O=Opportunity/objective
N=Nurturing
N=Nourishment
E=Equal/Evident
C=Cumulative
T=tantalizing/Tolerance
I=Inventive/Innovative
O=Open/Optimistic
N=Natural/Neutral

To join
Or combine
Relatability
Sharing
Healthy or dysfunctional
Interdependent or codependent
Self
Others
Nature versus Nurture
Fixing/Rescuing
Feeding or depleting
It is up to me to decide what type of connections
I choose to have

"Crevices"

The cracks on the street contain the smallest particles
Small creases between my mouth were locked tight as a child
Secrets were required to be kept
Cult-like
Quiet society under the roof
Dressing up nice and neat for the public
Presenting as one thing
Skin peeling back revealing the truth
The muscular structure was not seen by the family
The veins bulging with tainted blood
Heart cold as a glacier
Ice Queen
Your words and touch altering my life
Making me hypothermic
Heart barely beating
It did not stop your advances
The hair on the back of my neck standing up
Cringing at the thought of you

Violation
Foul
Intentional clipping, or was it?
No boundaries

What you wanted/needed is what you took
Stealing my innocence
My purity
The original me
Lack of freedom
No choice then

Just your grubby hands
Manipulating my mind and body
I am left to piece the puzzle together
To find my way back to me
Past your fingertips
The soap and water could not be away

"Prayers"

Prayers felt unheard and lost in the air
They left in a thought bubble
In hopes for something or someone to read or hear
To feel the agony they captured
It was usually in the form of prayers
The adults would recite
Praying to their God seemed unnatural
Like a lie
Their God did not create me
It was a facade and powerful over me
I did not trust prayers to that God
I knew no other God
So I tried to bed for safety and security
It never came

Their God had failed me again and again
Please help me
Fix the grown-ups
They are hurting me
According to them
You are hurting me too
Who else can I pray for help from?

There was no one or anything, so I thought
I felt a power greater than me around me

It was never my entity to pray to
It was theirs
I did not trust or believe I would get a release
So I denied and ran from
A power greater than myself

As I got older, I ran faster
Avoiding a connection or relationship
No longer wanting to feel unworthy and less
than
Gravitating to other types of prayers
Nothing changed
I was still that wounded child
Full of fear and shame

Believing I was shame and a bad girl
No longer that little girl
She still resides in me
Buried alive by the pain and trauma she endured
Crushed by fear, pain and anger
Just wanting to feel the air
On her skin
The sun in her eyes
And peace in her heart

“Boundaries”

Pleasing people for approval
Seeking people to pity instead of love
Insecurities and inner critic
Lost in the inside to the out
Looking for someone to fill the void
And fix me or
I fix them
Always love a project

A project to be responsible for
To care for, in my passive-aggressive way
How can I help?
What can I do?
Are you ok?
I suggest that you do this or that
Because I knew what was best for others
Or at least I liked to think

Resentment sets in
Gossip and disrespect
Exact replica of my life
Growing up in a family of chaos and disarray
Definitely not leading with love

Broken-hearted
Living in the sand
Self-protection
Value of self
Shows my inner children there is a different way
I’ve got you
You deserve it all
I can protect you my loves
Never alone

"Monopoly"

The board was so immaculate
Colorful and demeaning all in one
Possibility of jail if not careful
Rules modified by people I was playing with
Strategic and aligned to have an advantage

The streets signified the poverty and wealth
Boardwalk and Park Place were above the
paygrade
People would lose a limb to get these properties
I gravitated towards Baltic and Mediterranean
Ave.
They signified what was familiar
Relatability was always the goal

Railroads whistled loudly and caught my
attention
Must get all 4 so I can tax my opponents
Utilities were essential
Seeking both so they had to roll the dice and
multiply

Passing go to collect $200.00 each time
Some did not agree with this rule
The monies were coming from the bank
No harm no foul

Anxiously awaiting my turn
I sought to buy as many properties as I could
Also not wanting to spend all my money doing
so

The thimble and car were the top choices
Racing the car down each street
Hoping to outrace my competitors
A game of negotiation and bargaining
The goal was to annihilate everyone
To be the last one standing

It was more than a game
Often resembled my living situation
The people who I shared the same DNA with
The disease of family dysfunction was
destroying us all
Pushing us deeper and deeper into codependence
I was often trying to figure out how to
Navigate the board game of my own life.

"Face Down"

Face down in the dirt
Dust and pebbles going up my nose
Tears filling the eyes
Trickling down the cheek
Coughing from the ground and her eyes leaking
Laying her spotted face to die

The bottom is here
Dragging her down
Scraping the knees against the gravel
Belly full of cuts and bruises
Universe please help me
Laying her spotted face to die

Asking for help is out of my comfort zone
It has to be done
No more hopes and dreams
Just a reality that looks bleak
Laying her spotted face to die

Then a warm breeze blows against her face
Drying up the tears
The sun gets brighter
Spreading the vitamin D on the skin
Replenishing what has been lost
Giving a different energy in the atmosphere

Soft melody playing in the background
Unconsciously forcing the head up
Out of the dirt
Toward the beautiful sky
Pushing up on her knees
Feeling a sense of calmness
Taking over the body
A new sensation
Head up
Chest up
Peacefully breathing
Glimpses of relief and happiness
Hopeful there can be more moments like this

"Equity"

Have the scales ever been balanced?
Is the level of care working to preserve life?
Promote success?
Differences not promoting hatred?
Challenging the system of inequity
Centuries of dismay of them
Projecting fears onto others
But still the powerful control
Attacking from every angle
Treated worse than Cujo when he had gone mad
Slaughtered, captured, identity ripped away
Any fluctuation of hue to the skin

Criminal system, education, and housing
Are just a few examples
Neighborhoods impoverished
Living conditions horrific
Education system preparing students for less than
Strategically creating divide
Do all students receive free and APPROPRIATE education?
Are people afforded the same opportunities?
History and present-day show a similar trend

Criminal justice system biased and jagged
"Books" being thrown toward people with
darker skin tone
Hush before you are punished
Accused of being violent and aggressive
Compared to wild animals
Viewed as less than human

Fright is contagious and insane
Breathing the air
Drinking the Kool-Aid
Burned at the stake and stoned
Lynched and drowned
Year 1955, Mississippi, Emmet Till
Gone too soon
In 2022, 38 transgender people were fatally shot
or killed in a violent way
Police brutality
Will it ever end?!

“Woulda, Coulda, Shoulda”

Use your brain. That is why God gave it to you!

How many times do I have to repeat myself?

Who do you think you are?

What did I tell you to do?

Why aren’t you doing it yet?

Why aren’t you doing it right?

What’s between your ears? Air?

Here we go again!

Do as I say, not as I do

What happened to your hair? You look a mess.

I told you so!

I’ll give you something to cry about

Don’t ask me. You figure it out.

You are going on a diet because I am not buying you new clothes anymore!

You need to work out!

Get over yourself

What's funny?

It's all in your head

Don't flatter yourself

Here we go again
You can do better than that

What else were you expecting?

I told you to close your mouth!

Close it or I will close it for you!!

You haven't had the right man yet

Get over it!

No one cares!!

“Cheers”

The glass clanking
Not breaking
Celebrating howls across the room
Smiles on faces
Dressed to the nine
Bow ties and tuxedos
Ball gowns and updos
Elegant but quaint
Noses at equal levels
Feels elaborate and fancy
But there is another vibe underneath
The drums beat louder
The air is thicker
Making it hard to breath
Inhale deeply
Exhale slowly
Memories flooding like a mudslide
Spirits speaking clearly
Unable to be seen
Reminiscing about their lives
So desperately needing to be heard
PLEASE…….. Save me

“Mi Casa”

Mi means my
Casa means home
Su means you

Welcome to Mi Casa
Excuse the clutter
It is lived in
The atmosphere is zen
Sage burning to clean the energy
Killing germs and undesired juju

Wood floors from the 1950s
In pristine condition
Walls white with pieces of art
Inviting and calm, until it wasn’t
Usually peaceful and relaxing

Aroma lingering outside on the street
Home cooking straight from the garden
Mouth watering for dinner
Kitchen is a playground of fun, creation, and joy

The backyard is large and green
Vegetables and fruit growing
The lawn is freshly mowed
Birds chirping
Squirrels watching me as I sit on the deck
A family of squirrels

Watching my every move
What bradley little eyes you have
I share my space with all of my higher power's creatures

Walking barefoot in the grass
Getting grounded with Mother Nature
Helps me connect to my true parent
Different forms of creations and life
Right in the yard
Biology all around

Trees bright with green leaves
Woodpecker tapping at its home
Rabbits dodging cards and humans
Searching for food and shelter

Children playing outside
People walking their pets
Waving as they walk by
Neighbors speaking kindly to each other
Cars driving by with music bumping

The sun glistening against the skin
Thank goodness for sunblock
Pigment getting darker as I play
Basking in the beauty
Absorbing the natural vitamin D
Higher Power, thank you for mi casa and su casa

"Mother Nature"

The yard was small in stature
It is filled with ever-growing life
Every inch has Mother Nature touching it
I feel that same energy
The green grass grounding me to the earth
The bright blue/purple grapes growing on the fence
My grandmother in her moo-moo
Bent over at the waist
Bone cracking and crunching
The dirt was cool to the touch
Worms were fat and juicy
Abundance existing in the small space of her backyard
Greens were thick and bright
Green bean pods filled with nutrients

A closeness happened in that garden
A feeling of safety and freedom
Skills were being taught and absorbed
The skin was ingesting the air and sun
Bringing a shimmer to my skin
Enhancing my melanin
Hot to the touch
Sunscreen was sometimes used

Been burnt by the sun
Even to my surprise
Peeling after a few days
Worth every layer of dead skin
A sense of calmness
Filled my cut-up
Serenity at its finest
Peace on earth became real in those few hours
Now that I can see clearer
I have gratitude for those moments and seek
more

“Bookbag of Pain”

A photo of the family tree
Wrinkled and faded
Full of secrets

A piece of a gum wrapper
Crumbled up in a tiny ball
Doublemint and Juicy Fruit were the worst

An old umbrella that is ½ broken
I get soaked in the rain
Not allowed to get a replacement

Class books, notebooks, and calculator
The struggles of math in high school
If I don’t stay on top with a C,
No freedom will be allowed

Favorite pair of gym shoes
Thankful for my job
Mom was not paying

Independence in a bag
Full of good times and trauma
Growing faster than a child should

I have carried you
Even when I was not going to any classes
Been around for 50-plus years

Some things are a pleasure to carry
Others no longer have a purpose
They are obstacles

Prohibiting me to have autonomy from the old days

“Mickey Mouse Photo”

I see you Mickey with your red tongue sticking
out
Big hand on my shoulder
Cute yellow bowtie
Ears bigger than I would have ever imagined
Looking back at the picture
You seemed short in size
I am smiling
Eyes staring at something or someone
Could it be you?
Sponge curler as my bang with a white ribbon
It’s like a halter top with green straps
Tied around my neck
Whiter bow ribbon in my ponytail
Blue sunglasses hooked onto my top
The Mickey Mouse pin right above
Such a small thing
Innocent and full of life
Wide-eyed
Florida was a yearly destination for us
To this day, I still like Florida
But even there, the truth was still with me

“All The Things”

Why not?
What is wrong with having desires?
Not settling?
Exploring the explorable
Sharing connections
Living outside the boxes
Being aware of my intentions
Leading with transparency and authenticity
Navigating my life on my own terms
Strangling the voices of past and present
All is for me to decide
Who do I want to have in my life?
What capacity?
Peeling back the layers of the onion
Exchanging
Complimenting each other
Giving and Receiving
Interdependent
What I see is best for me
How I want it
Permission-based communication
Only allowed
Shooting straight from the hip
All parties able to speak their truth
Each individual
Personal in their own regard

Rawness is most attractive
Realness is stimulating
Eye contact traveling deep within
Words mingling with each other in the air
Skin grazing against each other
Holding hands
Humor captivating the room
Laughs consuming the sadness
Tears releasing pain
Spiritual connections
Sharing a page
Covered in a different script
Enhancing each other
Being seen and heard
Accepted and cherished
For just being oneself
Depicts love in all the ways I value
This is a story of my love for myself and others

"Raggedy Ann and Andy"

The dolls were custom-made
They were of darker complexion
My mother had them made for me, but also for her
She had purchased a beautiful crib for them
I love the smell of woods
Was also intrigued about having black stuffed dolls
Growing up, dolls of color were not as present as lighter-toned dolls
They were hand-stitched and vibrant
It was as if they were her dolls
She may have wanted them when she was younger
She took great pride in these abiotic factors
I thought she cared so deeply for them

It was unique to see that type of care and concern for an object
It allowed me to see a side of her that I did not see very often
The care she put into them
The concern she expected me to offer them
I was able to catch a glimpse of a glow
It was weird, scary, and surprising
It appeared to come from an authentic place

A place that was safe, fun, and light
The opposite of how I felt in my own skin
Makes me think….
She may have suffered in similar ways
Never seeing her love and attend to something with intent
It was a moment I humanized her

“Toolbox”

Full of hammers, nails, and screws
The hammer may be cracked
The nails may be bent
The screws are stripped
How can I use my tools when they are broken?
Are there other tools available to rebuild myself?
Where is the plaster and putty knife?
I need it
There are cracks in the foundation
Hand me the crack tape
So I can lay the putty on top
Can I borrow your saw?
The blade of mine is rusted
Will you give me a hand?
Please…
Will you hold the ladder?
As I climb to the top
Steady…
Thank you for your support
I can’t do it alone
Balance is a tool in the reconstruction of my life
The pandemic tipped the scale for many people
It may have been too heavy of a stressor
The toolbox almost empty
Others may have bounced back
Or were enslaved by the world changing

We are humans with different experiences and
tools
Some have tools that may not work anymore
Leveling out the scale can provide stability and
security

"Death"

The wind whips through my hair
Standing up tall like a soldier in the military
Trying not to blink or breathe
For that breath might be the last
Taking in as much oxygen as my lungs can hold

What will my last inhale feel like?
My breathing has changed through the years
Fast and furious
As if my heart was jumping out of my skin
Holding my breath
Short and shallow, like I was hyperventilating
More recent
Deep, thoughtful, and peaceful
Each and every day
My respiration can and has changed
The goal is to find balance and faith in each last breath

“Balancing Act”

A 100-foot tightrope without a balancing pole
A seesaw with weights only on one side
The Toyota without the starter
My neighbor who lost their job during the
pandemic
Virtual learning for students
Lack of child care for parents and caregivers
Elderly people dying at astronomical rates
People near and far
Affected by the same set of circumstances
Lack of connectivity with other people
No closeness or escape
Caught in the middle of the raging fire

What other life-altering things have happened?
We all have a story
We are similar, more than different
But my experience since the fetus
Have shaped my abilities and deficits
Wounds that have ever been shown or shared
UNTIL NOW…

The toolbox is needed
A hammer and nails to secure the parts
Thick wood for stability
Shingles to provide protection overhead

Drywall to enclose the most precious things
Insulation to keep us warm

All these items are ways to provide protection
Support
And Safety
It helps balance the scales
Providing a sense of comfort for some, not all
The box allows me to have stability
So adversity does not take over my life

"Who Am I"

A question that does not have just one answer
Complex but yet so simple
An infectious laugh and clap
They would startle a herd of elephants a mile
away
Bubbly and fun at the core
Scarred by trauma and abuse
Hiding behind the curtains
Wondering when it would ever be safe

What is safety?
Is it personal and/or societal?
Who is/was responsible?
To protect some of the most endangered species
Women, children, people of color, and queer
people

Often used and objectified
Getting hit over the head
Never seeing the hammer coming
No time to duck and dodge the heavy destroyer
How do we prepare to be exploited?
The plan has been in motion for centuries
Strategically placed in motion by the master
chess players
Always three moves ahead

Oppressing women, children, queer people, and any other minority group

“Strength”

The senses are powerful instruments
The sense of touch, smell, hearing, taste, and sight
Even when a person is not able to use all of them
The other senses become heightened
They give us presence
A stance in the world
Opportunity to create history from our own body
Transferred from within to the world
What a powerful set of tools
To enlighten the universe of our existence
Your perspective, your viewpoints, feelings, and emotions
Despite agreement; just freedom
Outside the societal parameters
Not confined to the box that many want to keep us in
Individuality and autonomy are a fight in this country
Too many want to gag and bind us
Make us pets, servants, and machines
Mindless and robotic
We are more
They are afraid of the strength we have
The acceleration of power from people
Who were thought to be less than

Unity evokes change
Acceptance promotes love
Love is freedom

"Scissors"

The scissors were one of my favorite tools
A sharp and large pair is the best
The ones that did not take too much precision
Keen enough they could snip the skin open
Where could I find a good sharpener?
They were in the drawer in the kitchen
I am sure you would never give me permission
To use them without your knowledge and close
eye
The bangs of hair had to go
I had to be meticulous and strategic
The perfect time would be when I was home
alone
In my head, I asked, "Is it worth it?"
Will she notice the change?
It was worth the risk to me
Snip, snip, snip
My hair falls to the floor
Panic ran through my body
What was done was done
No turning back
I played with the pieces of hair
Thoughts…..
Where am I going to hide the hair?
If she finds it, I am doomed
There was no turning back

"I understand your curiosity"
"I know you want independence teen"
"It will grow back"
"That was so creative, but these scissors are so razor sharp"
"I would not want you to hurt yourself"
"I will take you to get your haircut by a professional"
"You can pick your hairstyle"
Responses from a loving parent
Not the response I received

“Dear Higher Power of my mother”

I am writing to you to ask you to hold space for my mother. I never thought I would get to this point in my life, but I am thankful to be here. I am feeling more compassion and identifying with what compassion really is. I was at my recovery writers meeting last Friday. The writing shared was a piece to the higher power of the parent from the child's perspective. I broke down crying during the reading of the piece. So many emotions and feelings came up for me. I was surprised because anger has always been at the forefront of my emotions when it came to my mother. Despite it all, I loved her through it all.

As I got older, the programming that was done obligated me to love you even when you were causing me harm. As an infant or even in the womb, I was born in and with love. I am love. That love has been buried with the boulders that lay on top of my pure heart.

Mom’s god, please give her a place with nature, birds, animals, and plants. When I was growing up, she had several plants and a few birds. I remember finches. I also remember she and my father were interested in classic cars and motorcycles. We would frequently go to the race track and watch drag races.

I ask that she have a place to rest. In looking back, it never seemed she was able to rest (emotionally or physically). She was a hard worker and provider. Peace was not a feeling in the house growing up. Neither one of us had peace. I hope she is healed and in a place of peace. I still hold anger and fear. At times I want her to suffer, but I am coming to accept that she could not be any different than she was. I do not know the trauma and experience she endured. I am not sure what else she may want or need. You are her god and already know what is best for her. I still love her. I have had evil thoughts of punishing things I wanted her to go through, but looking back, she had suffered enough. Please hold and take care of her.

Love Tamara

"Hello Fear"

Dear old friend,
We have been together for such a long time
There were times I was all consumed by you
Unable to breathe
Gritting and grinding my teeth
The weight of the world on my chest
Crushing my little one's ribs and heart
I understand where and why you are so
prominent in my life
There was a time and place for you
I do appreciate how you helped us survive

Now, I am no longer a child/teen under the care
of the family
I am an adult still responding to things like a
child
It is not serving me any longer
I'm becoming more reliant on myself
Instead of expecting others to "fix" me
It is time for you to get some rest
I love and thank you.
I release your so I can get to me

“Holding my breath”

The floor was always filled with landmines
Mixed so delicately with shards of pieces of glass
Tiptoeing and holding my breath
Afraid to exhale too quickly
Easing in my footing with eyes peeled

You were always there, even when you weren’t physically there
Surveillance around the clock
Monitoring my every move
Taking up space in my mind, body, and soul
Afraid to exhale too quickly

Looking over my shoulders
Scared to fall asleep
Getting up to use the restroom
Tiptoeing and holding my breath
Attempting to rest, but can not rest with one eye opened

Morning shower before school
Here you come
No privacy
No need for assistance
I am old enough

But afraid to exhale too quickly
My heart racing as if I was running a sprint
Wishing I was running that sprint
In the opposite direction of you

I would not have stayed away too long
Because you were always in my mind, body, and
soul
Tiptoeing and holding my breath
Returning home to the roller coaster ride that
never stopped

Motion sickness and on high alert
Afraid to exhale to quickly
Feeling like my stomach was always dropping
Balance you say
What idea is this?
Completely foreign to my vocabulary

"Cinda"

Father, who is this woman you have brought into my life?
She is not my mother; oh how I miss thee
Your kindness and comfort
And your inner peace
Stepmother is quite the opposite

She is oppressing, jealous, and demeaning
I am enslaved to this pseudo-family
Yearning to be with my original, loving family

Forced to servitude
I must obey my stepmother
And my wicked step-siblings
They are put on a pedestal
While I am as low as the dirt
Being stepped and spit on
Called ugly and unworthy

Despite the horrendous reality
I drifted away in my mind
To a place where you still are mother
And when father was available to me
A place where dreams can come true

Breaking free from this prison
No longer an object at the disposal of others
Now a caterpillar in my cocoon
Awaiting the right season to be able
To transform into that beautiful butterfly

No holds barred
Me and the air
Sorrowing ever so freely
No longer on my hands and knees
Able to lift my head high in the clouds
Where dreams do come true

When will my fairy tale become my reality?
When the opportunity arises
You will be able to take full advantage of the life
you have always deserved

"Butterfly"

Emerging from a caterpillar to a butterfly
Transforming overtime
It takes time
To be able to fly
I started by crawling
Now I am ready to take-off
It did not happen overnight
Creating my own flight plan
Soaring and migrating
Sometimes with my tribe
Other times solo
Feeling the wind on my tiny wings

Pollinating the milkweed
Feeding myself and the world
Something to offer
Always enough
Even when I did not think so

Finding my way around the world
My beautiful colors
Illuminating the sky
The pattern is different from another other
My identity
My fingerprint

Navigating in a new way
Learning the safest paths to travel
Allowing others their own path
Thanking the universe for all of its gifts

“The Other Bag”

My backpack is a glossy black. It has patches and pins of some of my favorite music artists. Different genres of music. It also has some dark images. Like a tornado with black clouds. It represents the things that I carry around. There are some things I want to unload and other things that I cherish. It is a unique bag, personalized just to fit me.

“Sneaky Little Monster”

Sneaky and resilient
Consuming all the parts
Questioning everyone and everything
A pillow covering my face
As I try to rest easy
An elephant sitting on my chest
I feel it caving in
I can’t get it off of me

I squirm and flail like a fish out of water
Gasping for air and relief
Years and years of torment
“Tricky little monster”
Bestowed upon me by those closest to me
Trapped in my DNA

No choice but to own and fear it
Declaring war with no weapons
Chasing my tail like Tom on Tom and Jerry
Exhausted, but never defeated
Not giving up in this body

Following the path of denial has led me here
To a place and space where I can clear the fog
from my lenses
Still steamy at times, but I can still see
The beautiful light shining in
Even on the darkest days

“Bare”

Came into the world naked
Living in the womb
Surviving off of here energy, oxygen, and nutritions
Also absorbing the trauma she sustained in her life
Attached to the umbilical cord
Cushioned by the amniotic fluid
Growing in the fetal position in her belly
What an intense bond and form of connectivity
Sharing the DNA of mother, father, and all the generations
Almost innocent and pure
In the sac created by a power greater than myself
Naked and unafraid
Truthful and disrobed
Entering the world in my rawest and truest form

"Hide and Seek"

What a familiar game from my childhood
It was played among the children in the family
And the neighborhood kids
We played in houses
Or outside in the weather

It could be a sunny, rainy, or even snowy days
Concealing myself behind a tree
Or even climbing a mulberry tree
Hiding under a car, but trying not to get dirty
Teaming up with a friend or family member
Ducking seekers

What a rush of excitement and fear all rolled up into one
Scared to get caught
But hoping someone is looking for me
Attaching my value to the seeker
Deep down wanting to be missed or wanting to be found

After a period of time
I would get sad if no one looked
Feeling abandoned and alone
Wondering who was sought first
And why wasn't I?

It started out with joy and happiness
In a matter of minutes
It would turn into a lonely scenario
Wishing someone would find me already

"Space"

Once upon a time
In an urban city in the midwest
There lived an innocent caramel girl
She lived with her mother
The only child
The father gone by age 3 or 4 ish
The child has a bubbly spirit and full of laughter
Their smiles would brighten the gloomiest day
Nothing could dim their shine
At least they thought…even if only temporarily

As she/they grew more aware of the world and
her household
It felt incorrect, tormenting, caged, and unsafe
That grin became practiced instead of natural
Trying to find a way to get back to those bright
shiny days
"Let's try this"
"Oh that did not work"
"How about this?"
She kept adjusting who she was for other people
Stepping further and further away from
herself…

Becoming what was projected onto her
Never a break
No space for self-awareness or identification

Their large heart felt so much pain
Shrinking with every insult, touch, and beating
Retreating inward
Locking the door tight
Begging and praying for it to end

It never did
The wounds were deep and bleeding out
Out of control
Wheezing and coughing

Unsure to ask for help
Grabbing a tourniquet to help stop the bleeding
Blood pressure decreasing rapidly
Shortness of breath
Barely able to keep my eyes open

Such an unfortunate story
For such a brave little person
They are a model of strength beyond their years
More powerful than anyone wanted her to know
Never alone on her journey
"I have always been with you"
Even when you thought nothing was
I will never leave you
And I will show you how to never leave yourself again

Love the Universe

"Friend or Foe"

Hearing the moans and groans
The complaints of those people
The ones I thought were so different from me
Using their tongues as tools of manipulation
My ears opened wide to the language
Finding my own interpretation of what was
being said
Not really listening but in the mind
Judging and condemning every word
Figuring out how to "fix" them
How fickle could I have been
Moving from person to person
And place to place
Harpe in hand ready to crucify them with my
words
The blade is sharp
Splitting the finest of hairs

The answers to your problems and worries
I had them!
Sadly mistaken
The solutions were not applicable to them
It was about me and my ego
Crowding the room and trying to take up all
The space and air
Circling left to right

Saying the words with a smile
Trying to convince the audience to buy what I seeking
The product was like a fictional character
Farthest from the truth
All I once knew and believed

The weapon was so keen
It was seductive and daunting
Luring us in
It glistened in the light
Shining and bright
A thing of beauty
But so deadly to you and I

"Love as a Battlefield"

Entering the war zone
Never prepared for battle
Love as a battlefield
Just a youngster in your care
Host on the frontlines
Love is a battlefield

Facing the enemy I loved unconditionally
Why did you hurt me so bad?
Ill-prepared and searching for shelter and safety
Why did you hurt me so bad?
Often thinking, what can I do to stop the pain?
Love is a battlefield
Why do you hurt me so bad?

Heart-broken into pieces, but full of love
I felt chained to your side
Never able to have room and space
No room to breathe
Suffocated with what you called love
Why do you hurt me so bad?

I am trapped by your love
Taught to believe feel love in this way
In your way
So scary, painful, and threatening

Love as a battlefield
Bruised on the inside and out

What was I supposed to do?
I am chained to your side
Unable to inhale or exhale without permission
Hiding deep inside myself
Never sharing who I really am—because
Love as a battlefield

An adult wanting and needing
someone/something
To replace the love you gave me as a child
Love as a battlefield
Still handcuffed to your side
Unable to break free

“Unholy”

Getting hot
Sweat dripping
Glistening in the moonlight
Smoldering from the heat
Smoke fuming from the skin
Perspiration from me to you
Grab the fire extinguisher
Consensual between adults

Grasping and clawing
Sensual and seductive
All senses stimulated
Panting and moaning
Gratification and satisfaction
Goosebumps
Hair standing up
Blood flowing
Heart throbbing

Natural desire
Gift from the universe
Feeling alive
Why is it so taboo?
Connection between humans
Exploration using kissing, touching, smelling,
tasting, visually, and listening

Exotic and erotic

I claim holy
The essence of humanity
Lies in connection
Exchanging energy
Moving with love and kindness

“Distortion”

Tripping on the mushrooms
Seeing bright lights
When there is sadness
Perceiving fairness
When there is inequality
“Beaming up to Scotty”
When there is addiction all around
Floating on a cloud of delusion
When the world is imploding
Swimming in rubies and riches
When people are choking on poverty
Fast money seemingly tantalizing
When people are being sold as property
Passing the drink
The needle
The blunt
To solve the pain
These are ways the world has shown love to my
people and
How my people have shown love to each other

"Is It Mine?"

Mind, Body and Soul
Who do they belong to?
Is it mine?

The hands, eyes, and objects violated me
Undressing me
Exposing me
Robbing my stages of development
Is it mine?

Acts happening
Swept under the rug
Never a conversation
Things just being as they were
No explanation
Is it mine?

Gagged and bound
Force and coerced
Treated as a thing
Feeling less than
Puppeteered
Is it mine?

I reclaim me; despite my tragedy. I am not my past and my past was never me!!

“Down and Out”

D-destitute, debris, darkness, and desperation
O-overturning, overtly, opening, and ownership
W-women, whirlwind, weeping, and wiped
clean
N-nucleus, nuisance, neglect, and nepotism

Low, below, under, less than, without

O-outstanding, oppression, and opposing
U-understood, unwanted, and used
T-traumatic, tumultuous, and talented

No more closets, underground railroads. Taking
off the masks.

“The People”

I can give you everything you need
I know what you want and desire
Follow my lead
I can tell you who you are
What you like
Your value
And what you deserve
I can give you your identity
Come
Follow me
I will open the box
The door is wide open
Enter
Close the door behind you
The rules are written on the wall
Pay close attention
This is the only way to live
The ticket to the heavens
Your gift from (their god)
Be led
Or be lost
Lost forever
No pearly white gates for you

“Dreams”

Closing my eyes
Wondering if my eyes will open up again
The darkness causes panic
Nightmares were made at night while I slept
The dreams occurred during the light
Fascinated with physical strength
Bodybuilders, gladiators, and/or powerlifters
They were the deities I adored
Role models
Flex Wheeler
Storm from the American Gladiators
Being an Olympian
Track & Field was the jam
Running fast
Throwing weights
Wrapped up in the magazines and movies
Dissociating into the fantasy
Escapism
The ultimate dream was to be the opposite of
what I was born into

“Tam boy”

Never wanting to expose my figure
The bagger, the better
Loved overalls
Jogging pants
Oversized shorts
Bow ties and neckties
Jumpers
MC Hammer pants
Hiding all the feminine parts of myself
Hats and visors

“You look like a boy”
“You will never get a man”
“You are such a tomboy”

Climbing trees
Playing sports
Wanting to urinate standing up
All equated to never being able to get a man
According to them
To me…I was just Tam
Attempting to salvage personal boundaries and my body

“Hidden Tension”

Walking stiff like a robot
Arms swaying outward
Attempting to take up physical space
Head held high
Chest up and out

Do you feel it?

Hips holding stress from today and the trauma of yesteryears
Muscles surrounding my pelvis are short and tight
Tough like a tennis ball with all the tight rubber bands
Shoulders and back tight like a steel rod

Do you feel it?

Pain on top of pain
Year after year
Denying it in the moments
Ignoring my mind, body and spirit

Do you feel it?

Not knowing how to breathe to loosen the tension
Holding my breath as if I am in fight, flight, freeze, or fawn
50 years later, the body endures the cumulative physical, mental and emotional
Tucked away in the tissue

Do you feel it?

Screaming and kicking
Treating the symptoms with people, places and things
Recreating the aches and hurt

Do you feel it?

Mood affects on a daily basis
Tossing and turning in the sleep
Body reacting to the maltreatment
Unsure of what I was doing

Do you feel it?

The root of the tension surrounds hurt, pain, guilt, and shame
Deep beneath the surface
Projecting outward and inward

How can I help?
Do you feel it?

"Intellect"

Spent a lifetime studying
The geometry formulas
MLA and APA formats for papers
Sewing for beginners
Typing on the old school typewriters
Criminology
Special Education
Reading Comprehension
Literate and figurative writings
Do they really matter?

Developing intellect about people
Figuring out how to play chess with one chess piece
ME

Am I allowed to move diagonally like the Queen?
Or was I just the pawn?
Did I need the King?
Was it the fairy tale version
Or the one that no longer lived with me?
FATHER

Studying the facial expression
Body language
And glances

I never knew I needed a Ph.D. in
Just being ME

"Nourishment, or the lack thereof"

Waking up in the morning starving
Heading to bed malnourished
Feeling depleted
Can I have a piece of that pretty red watermelon?
I need it for hydration
My body is dehydrated
I am so thirsty
I have cotton mouth
Please ……as an evil look hits my eyes
Still waiting for my body to be replenished

I hear the grease popping in the kitchen
I smell the fish frying in the skillet
You know how much I love fried catfish
You enjoyed tilapia
But Grannie got me hooked on that catfish
The face with whiskers
Purring like a cat
Wiggling in the container before they take their last breath
Known as the bottom feeders
The roaches of the ocean
What unique health benefits that unique fish has

It can provide my body protein and essential
vitamins/minerals
My body craves them

Will you share the catch
Or will you hog it for yourself?
I have been waiting for years for that delicious,
fatty, crispy-skinned delicatessen

“Black”

Black is a word that I perceived to be negative
The world has devalued people of color
The darker the person
The more difficulty
The deeper the struggle

History has beaten us down with heavy fists
Like the sticks hitting that snare drum
Not allowed to look or stare

Expected to be property
And do as we are told
Being objectified
For others to use at their expense
For the right price

Now we have become our own worst enemy
Killing
Torturing
Drugging
And selling each other to the highest bidders

What if
We joined together?
Thrived together
Lived together

No longer serving

Making more opportunities
For ours and others
Less fortunate
Spreading more love
Kindness and joy
Learning from past errors
Caring for each other
Encouraging one another

How differently we could see each other
Human to human

"Gated"
There is a fine line in the sand
Walking a tightrope
Learning to juggle one egg at a time
Walking on a frozen river

Being aware of the delicate water
The faded line on the beach
It sometimes can move from the waves washing
on shore
I can forget where the lines were

Slowly dipping my toes in the ocean
One foot at a time
Uncertain when the bottom will drop

Not the best swimmer
Tiptoeing
Inching
Prayer for nature to guide me

Building a beautiful fence
Enclosed with a lavish gate
Able to come in and go
Available to whom I choose to let in
Careful Tamara

Sometimes we leave the gate open
Not knowing what or who to expect
It is easy to step into desire and being desired
The fear of abandonment runs deep in our
tissues

"The Clappers"

Longer than pinocchio arms
Commonly made of wood
Strings attached and manageable by the
puppeteer
Dangling
Clanking
Clapping
Creating sounds
Percussion
Beats and rhythms

Scratches on the forearms
Dents on the wrists
Holes drilled through the upper arms
Fingernails resembling mine

Enchanted with spiritual magic
Or weapons used for beheading
Slapping across the face
Or on the head
These tools have many uses
Just depends on the user

Healthy vs. unhealthy
All hands can be
Even wooden ones made in England

Self-inflicted or self-expressed

Curved from nature
By a set of hands
Intricate and deliberate
Intention and focus
Designed and displayed

The message is clear
Concise
The hands and arms can offer comfort to self
and others
Or they can leave scars deep in the tissue
Taking an eternity to attempt to heal

Does one choose music for healing
Or trauma to cause deep pain
Or both
It is entirely up to us

"Dreadful"

I often felt an intense fear of being near my
mother
I also felt angry
I wanted her to suffer at times
Never wanting to be around her as I grew up
Just her and I in the apartments
Too much time together
Riding a rollercoaster of fear, anger, and
uncertainty
Her shame, guilt, and never feeling worthy
Translated to the young me

Worthy?
Defined of value or importance
Can also be a last name
And it was
Assigned to the man that I did not grow up with
Never there to encourage or protect
Do not think you were able to do it anyway
But it would have been nice for you to have
been there
Or would it have been?
No clue
The kid me wanted you there

The children in me were always wanting someone to rescue them
From all pain, abuse, torture
My mother was my primary caregiver
Who cared for me in ways that were harmful
My father was missing in action
The extended family appeared fearful of her
Just like I was
No one questioned or challenged the vessels that bore me

Even when I was away from her
I dreaded the thought of going back to her
All my hair standing up on my arms and the back of my neck
So many things happened
Many things happened that I can not recall
Part of me is thankful for that
The other part still feels the pain embedded in my muscles
I do remember feeling terrible feelings
As an adult, I carry the abuse and trauma from years ago
Undealt with decades
Affecting my mind, body, and soul
I had some relief when she passed away
Did not have to worry about looking over my shoulder
Or running into her at a grocery store

Avoided certain places so I would not have to
see her
I can feel where I hold some of my trauma
I clench my jaws
Grind my teeth, especially at night when
sleeping
My jaw, neck, upper and lower back, and my
genital
Hold the pain
It has been an eye-opening experience to be able
to accept what has happened
And learn ways to move forward with my life
I am here because of all the things
Starting to see and embrace my worthiness
And getting to my whole self

“Unknowns”

Uncertainty can cause fear in people
Each and every day has unknowns
What is the approach?
To maneuver what we don’t know is coming
Is it isolation, seclusion, or hiding?

Opening the window even though there is a storm outside
Spreading my arms open wide to receive what is being given
Embracing the gifts of nature each day
Thanking my higher power
Providing nourishment for all things on the earth
The Queen Mother of My World

She shares her love through the plants, humans, animals, and natural disasters
Sweeping in like a tsunami
Destroying all in its path
Not person, just
Life ends for all
Life is not forever on this planet

They are resilient, but to a fault
Not asking for support or help
Self-reliant and drained

Unable for herself or others
Tapped out; just like society expects

She does not get time to care for herself
Because what she knows is what she does
Sacrificing to do EVERYTHING
For EVERYONE
Excluding herself
The list is never-ending

Arms length and growing
Surpassing my upper body
Draping on the floor
How much can I endure?
Not the thoughts that cross my mind

How do I ask for help?
If I ask, how do I accept the help?
I like to think I have all the answers
Clearly, I have no clue about these two questions
History states I am nothing and less than
I believed in that history for the major of my life
My highest power tells me I am everything
A part of it
From the beginning

Just starting to believe it

"LIFE"

How do I want my existence to be?
Never really thought about it honestly
At least from a realistic space
I have thought about from a delusional space
I just wanted to be someone or something to remove the pain
I never thought I was able to do it myself

I would like my life to be led with courage and self-love
I have been courageous
And unfamiliar with the love piece
I want the fears of the unknown and people to dissipate
I want to find my freedom in a way that does not revolve around
The illusion of control, manipulation, reacting, and being a victim
I am no longer a victim

I want to feel safe and able to create healthy boundaries for myself
I want to be able to explore life, connections, and experiences
I have had many thoughts and dreams that I thought were unattainable

I want to be present and open to the world
I have missed so many opportunities because I
have spent a lifetime
Wanting to get out of my body

“My WE”

The part has never been just me
There has always been a “thing”
That I connected too
Young and unsure
Afraid and unknowing
Saved my life before I knew what living was
Shielded me from the outside world
Created a space and traits
To help me survive
Never alone in the terror and insanity
You are the warm sun heating my skin
The air I breathe
The hope I yearn for

I didn’t always believe in you
The chaos helped me distort my thinking
How could “you” allow me to be?
The innocent in the den of wolves
A morsel to the hungry giants
I did not understand

‘We’ is the blanket you provided that others can not see
The ocean breeze
A community of ‘Us’
The vessels of humans

Pen and paper
Helping me see and define my true self

‘We’ also includes me
All the parts
Separated shortly after birth
Branching off
In the trenches
With the intention to protect that original me

I would not be here
Without me and we and you

"Losses"

Spending so many years together
Entangled
Codependent
Dysfunctional
Care and Concern
In our own ways
Not aligning
Attempting to control and manipulate one another
The past trauma of each
Woven together in another maze of madness
I felt I needed you
Needing others to fill my cup with all the things
I have missed my entire life
Ending with me clinging to the past
My way or the other way
Thanks for cutting the cord
I wish I would have handled things differently on my end

I can focus on the primary person in my life
That has been abandoned by me for decades
I have no hatred
I have gratitude
I wish you the best
Clarity is my friend

Acceptance is my truth
Denial is still in my tissues
I am working on releasing the inflammation

"Entanglement"

You began early in my life
Enmeshment
Cobb webbed
Intersecting line forced into my DNA
Not only yours, but all the people in my life
Never having a choice

Scripted as if I were in a broadway show
Performing the NutCracker
Or the marionette
The strings were not mine
They grew out of insanity

How can I cut through the maze
It has been injected deeply
Do this!
Do that!
Tugging-pulling
Contradiction and confusion

Where was I in all of this?
Deeply buried
Covered up like a mummy in the tomb
But still breathing and feeling
Alive, not well

Surviving, not thriving
Feeling stuck for several decades

Until now….
The true story has just begun

"Adaptation"

Sliding into other people's lives
Wishing and pretending
Believing that clothes people's family were healthier than mine
They seemed different
Or at least I thought they were
Were they performing like my family or I did?

It would seem peaceful but chaotic
Unique from my home
Some homes were infested with things
Others were cookie-cutter homes
The ones you might see in a Home & Garden magazine
The hedges perfectly shaped
Manicured by a lawn care service

Kids had voices, or so it seemed
The parents would laugh and joke with the kids
Mistakes were met with gentleness

Catholic church….in and out
Kneeling repeatedly
Not sure how the elders were able to keep up
Southern Baptist church….from sunup to sundown

Sunday School
Afternoon service
Then evening service
I pick Catholic church…please

Say the Hail Marys and all is forgiven
The slate is clean
At the family church, the bar could never be met
The mold was for all
Perception was my reality

“Blade”

The wounded son
DNA had been altered in the womb
Sustained trauma before entering the world
What mother felt, he felt her pain
It pumped through the veins and heart
The core of the child changed forever

Relatable unfortunately
Trauma has caused the deepest of wounds
At times, feeling they are unable to be healed
The world was the enemy
My family was the enemy
Forcing me to become something else
Just as they had become

I attempted to force others to be my loving parent
Using manipulation, people-pleasing, and “control”
Wanted to be chased, cuddled, and loved
Having no idea of what healthy looked like

Wanting others to feel the touch of Karma
Please let me watch

"Flowing"

The energy is stuck inside me
There is a blockage as if I am having a stroke
Grasping for oxygen; choking on carbon dioxide
Feeling like I am suffocating
Two hands squeezing my throat so tightly
That fear and pain so centered within

The other side has a light
A glimpse of life
Hope and evolution
Rotating on the axis
Tilting toward the sun
Offering nutrients and minerals across the land
Rearing animals and cultivating crops
Light as a cloud
The biggest cotton ball on the planet
Made of pure security, protection, and calmness

Letting the air get through those tight hands
On my throat
Releasing the forceful grip
The sunshine hits my face
Brightening my eyes, skin, and soul
Penetrating the core of my body
Raising my internal temperature
Almost too hot to touch

Smoke coming from those restraints around my neck

The energy entering my soul over other powers of the threat
Desensitizing the skin on the palms, but still very dry
To force sadness and pain onto me
But the energy flowing through me fights the battle
Fully armed to defend and protect that buried heart
At all costs
No price too high
No force too strong
I see the exhaustion on your face
Alone with the shame
I feel your suffering and start to cry
Seeing part of your story melt your strong face

No longer hard as a buck
Softened up
The steel exterior vanishing right before my eyes

“Dear Loving Parent (me)”

I would have never thought we would meet. What a pleasant surprise. I truly never even knew you existed; especially within me. I always expected my biological parents and others to be my loving parents. Unfortunately, the years of generational dysfunction, alcoholism, and lack of recovery, I went on a different course. Here we are. Meeting each other recently. I can say it is a pleasure, but it seems to be a lot of hard work

And it is. I can see your actions. They are more caring and from a place of understanding and love. Those younger parts of me receive it and other times do not trust it. They are not used to the gentleness or moderation you offer. They are used to reactiveness and imbalance in their lives. They are used to being hypervigilant, unsafe, afraid, fearful, and alone. They have never felt like they have had a voice or identity of their own. They have felt trapped and uncared for so long. My inner child and inner teenager were objectified, used, and disregarded. They are in need of freedom, love, compassion, reassurance, and patience. I am grateful for you.

“Good”

What is good?
Who gets to define it for me?
Is it desired?
Is it morally right?
Under whose rule of what is good?

Good has been a standard of achievement in my life
My family of origin had their version of good
I never met the standard
I desired their love, care, and safety
Three things they were ill-equipped to provide

Boor in an environment that felt like my world
Full of betrayal to the highest degree
Pain and suffering
But I was still full of the purest love
Unknowing
Waiting and wanting to share it
Getting lost along the way
She carried the heavy cloak on her back
Weighed down and often feeling defeated
Able to free herself from the restraints of the family
She entered the world
Frightened and clueless

Often drawn to that familiar torture
The innermost part had hoped and dreamed
And she even had faith
But in what?

A beautiful forest
Bright and green
Vibrant and thriving
Blooming and blossoming
Providing oxygen
Supporting life and existence
Showing her even in the harshest conditions,
Life still exists

"Hours of Exploration"

Hearing you breath
Ears perked up
Feeling it on my lips
So close, but not touching
It sends vibrations through our bodies
Traveling south
All the way to our toes
Inhaling your air
You inhaling mine
Sucking in deeply
Then we swallow

My hands speak a different language
Mind of their own
Heading around the back of your neck
Gradually sliding to the front
Applying light pressure
Lips locked together
Tongues dancing

You suck my tongue with just enough pressure
I open wide so you can get it all
Getting pulled in deeper
Falling into you
I request your tongue
Latching on with a firm grip with my lips

The moans increase
Smooth strokes back and forth
In sync
Bodies pressed together
I slowly let go

Back into your mouth it goes alone
Taking your lips with mine
Using my tongue to outline your lips
Then…kissing you passionately

Bodies jerking uncontrollably
Still fully dressed
Eyes closed
Smelling and kissing your neck
My arms wrapped around you tightly
Better grab your Timberlands

Shorter than you
And ready to climb that tree
Brace yourself……

“D.E.B.R.A”

I am the person whose egg participated in your life
It wasn't just me
The sperm donor was your father
He wasn't around much after the first few years
They say I kept him away from you
Maybe parts of me did
I was hurt and very much emotionally unavailable to everyone
We were you
I had you when I was 20 years old
No clue of what to do as my part
Even though I was one of the babysitters for my younger siblings

Born third oldest came with many responsibilities
There were eight, but one died early in life
I felt like a servant to my parents
Not having time for me
Any individuality and tons of pressure
It was like a pot boiling over

Never feeling like I was enough as a child
Doing my best each day of my life
But it was never what you deserved as my child

I had always been tough on you
I never let you breath
Same breath that was taken from me

My life was full of trauma that I never
mentioned
Keeping the family secrets was the unwritten
rule in the house
The same rule I taught you
I forced many of the same experiences on you
that I experienced
Not healthy or loving
Just was
Unfortunately......

“Vegetable Garden”

(This is about a person and a learning experience that offered me comfort, calmness, and life skills.)

Comfort was very difficult to find in my mother's house. For just the two of us living there most of the time, it always felt chaotic and tense. I cannot recall a time when I felt comfortable in her house.

At my grandmother’s home, I would find glimpses of safety and comfort. It was not a regular occurrence, but there were several moments. They were not consistent, but they stood out.

In the garden, weeding, planting, picking, and watering the foods of our labor. I felt the most peaceful and productive in the dirt. Using soil, plants, and seeds my Higher Power offers for life and nourishment. Contributing to the cycle of life. Getting my hands dirty. Tilling the rows; memories of Verna Mae in her moo moo, bending the incorrect way and hearing her say how much her back hurt. Imitating the way she was bent over (paying for it today). OUCH! Watching her movement and gentleness with the plants. Getting a lesson of what each item was that we were planting and harvesting. What great wisdom and care she put into her craft! Having seven children (one died at an early age), there were many mouths to feed. So many grandchildren and community people to provide nourishment for. Managing to conserve money that was often low or nonexistent.

The garden was so much more than some plants, herbs, veggies, and fruits. It was life. It was health, abundance, wealth (not the monetary kind), friendship, love, sharing, and caring. Many of the things that take a back seat in my mind because it is flooded with trauma. Thinking about these moments with my grandmother, reminds me of all the blessings, happy moments, and gratitude I often forget about in the day-to-day.

I learned so many life lessons and skills from my grandmother. She taught me how to filet and scale a fish. I lived, practiced, and performed farm-to-table living. I learned how to truly appreciate what God bloomed and provided for the family to survive.

She also taught me how to preserve and can fruits and vegetables to last us through the winter months. She grew enough crops to last the entire year. It also helped take some of the financial burden off of my grandparents.

“Farming As a Terrorist Act”

Pollination is an act of Mother Nature
Or as I choose to call my Higher Power
It is a force greater than myself or anything for that matter
Providing shelter and food for all living things

Farm to table
Holiday spreads
All available from what was given so freely
Until you came along like a wrecking ball
Heavy steel with greed stamped on the chains

Corporations and policy-makers taking what belongs to all of us
Destroying food sources, water supplies, habitats, and life
Polluting the air, water, and soil
Focused on the mighty dollar to stay in the majority

Suppressing the minority with your clad fist
Beating us over the head with the hammer
Knocking down trees to build more factories, companies, and housing developments
Overpriced for most
Dead end jobs

Global Warming and the Greenhouse Effect
The core of our beautiful planet getting hotter
and hotter

Seasons changing
Winter getting shorter
Summers are longer and scorching
The fall, oh how I have missed you
Cool air grazing my face
Leaves transitioning from all the greens
To the oranges, reds, browns, and then to the
ground you go

The pollinators becoming extinct
Farmers being inventive to create crops
Fit for humans, animals, and the rest of the
world
Not full of toxins and poison
Full of love with the intent to nourish the body
Instead of abolish

Fear-based thinking keeps them ahead of the
game
Afraid of not having a thumb on our necks
Trying to break our necks
At times it happens, but many are surviving
Some even thriving

“Exchange”

Beginning with a look
A glance
How long is the sharing?
What are the eyes saying at the moment?
Do you feel any heat?
What is being given and received?

Eye contact can be intimidating as well as probing
Such an intimate swap
Looking at color
Shape
Accessories around in the eyes
Are they gentle?
Do they question?
Do they look safe?

All the thoughts that can come up in a brief encounter
Gateway
Expressive
Dancing
Genuine
Uplifting
They can smile with joy

They can well up with tears
A very special sense

Revealing if one allows
Able to undress
Create an assumption with no evidence
Penetrating
Inviting
Vulnerability
Come inside

Show me who you are
Wanting to see past your exterior
Wanting to get to know who you are
Another level
Who are you at your original self?
That is what I want in my life
Are you able to show me?
Do you want to show me?
Am I able to show you?
Do I want to show you?

Do we have more than an initial physical connection?
Is there more?
How deep are we willing to go?
Life is short
I wanna dive in
Seep in through the skin

Show me how you live and love
Do we speak a similar language?
Are we kindred spirits?
Do our energies align?

It will take time
It can be easy
Communication and conciseness
Transparency
Willing to speak your deepest truth
Are you ready?

Take a deep breath
Exhale slowly
Let's take this ride
And see what we can see

Starting and ending with the eyes

“Frightening Slumber”

The evenings were dark
Not only dark from the time of day
But because of the energy in the house
Gloomy and evil feeling
Like I get from watching scary movies like Cujo
Anticipating the worst to come

Holding my breath and the pillow
Wishing it would all be over sooner than later
Curled up in the fetal position
In my bed
The place I thought I would have privacy
And be free to breathe and relax

The contrary happened
It was a place of violations, pain, fear, shame,
and lack of trust
The bedroom has haunted me
Just like I was a child all over again
But, the reality is, I am now an adult
No longer subjected to adults objectifying me
Or the adult me objectifying myself

9 789363 313446

Printed by Libri Plureos GmbH in Hamburg,
Germany